WHAT ONCE WAS THERE
IS THE MOST
BEAUTIFUL THING

✻

CATIE HANNIGAN

WHAT ONCE WAS THERE
IS THE MOST
BEAUTIFUL THING

✽

CATIE HANNIGAN

NEW MICHIGAN PRESS
TUCSON, ARIZONA

NEW MICHIGAN PRESS
DEPT OF ENGLISH, P. O. BOX 210067
UNIVERSITY OF ARIZONA
TUCSON, AZ 85721-0067

<http://newmichiganpress.com>

Orders and queries to nmp@thediagram.com.

Copyright © 2015 by Catie Hannigan.
All rights reserved.

ISBN 978-1-934832-50-9. FIRST PRINTING.

Printed in the United States of America.

Design by Ander Monson.

Cover image by Catie Hannigan.

CONTENTS

First Time Gone   1
Yard Sale/ Candle   2
Becoming   3
Feelings 101   4
A Message   5
A Reply   6
Devour   7
Winnowing   8
Defend Existence   9
New Mexico   10
[Vibrating]   11
Carpe Diem   12
Yard Sale/ Antlers   13
Contempt   14
Yard Sale/ Rumbottle   15
Her Death   16
Yard Sale/ Red Boots   17
Like a Seashell Before it Dries   18
Begging the Scenery   19
Pawn Shop   20
Yard Sale/ Sifter   21
The Painter   22
Yard Sale/ Tintype   23
Looming   24
Allowance   25

Itll Be Okay   26
No It Wont   27
Flush that Takes   28
Icestorm   29
Love I   30
Love II   31
Re-Naming the Beach   32
Yard Sale/ Lantern   33
When We Were Birds   34
Unremembering 1   35
Unremembering 2   36
Yard Sale/ Antlers II   37
North   38
Confused Ghazal   39
Receive/Perceive   40
Fury   41
Eyes or the Long Stare   42
For the Last Time   43
Yet to Say   44
[Wake Me]   45

Acknowledgments   43

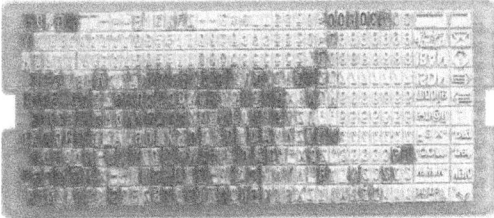

THIS WORK
WAS CREATED
USING ONLY A
2000 PLUS PRINTER 30
SELF INKING STAMP

FOR HANNA

FIRST TIME GONE

A CHORUS OF BELLS
CARRIES THE COWS THRU
THEIR QUIET.
DISTANCE WHIMPERS

YARD SALE/ CANDLE

                      THE SUN
                      PUCKERED
                      GOLD

BECOMING

A WAY THAT IS
NOT STOPPING
YOU NOT I

FEELINGS 101

SHOW
DONT
TELL

A MESSAGE

HOW COULD YOU

A REPLY

YOU
DID
IT
FIRST

DEVOUR

BEEN LOST
NOT UNLIKE DEATH
BY SORROWS
NOW OPEN

WINNOWING

I WANT
TO UNWANT
EACH TOUCH

DEFEND EXISTENCE

                    IT WILL PROVE ITSELF
                    TO YOU

NEW MEXICO

DAYS
DRIFT FAR.

VIBRATING
LINE
OF
BEING

CARPE DIEM

                    FUCK
                    MYSTERY

YARD SALE / ANTLERS

SPLITTING TIME
BETWEEN ARMS
OF BONE

CONTEMPT

        COME OUT
         COME OUT
        WHEREVER
        YOU ARE.

YARD SALE / RUM BOTTLE

                RINGING
                AS A PENNY
                DROPPED
                I AM

HER DEATH

YARD SALE/ RED BOOTS

                WOULD SHE
                HAVE WORN THEM
                IF NOT
                FOR HIM?

LIKE A SEASHELL
BEFORE IT DRIES

                                        DEPENDING ON THE LIGHT
                                        YOU MAY
                                        FIND ME
                                        MORE BEAUTIFUL

BEGGING THE SCENERY

        A GUST
        A GASH
        NOT YOU
        OR FLEETING
        YOU

PAWN SHOP

WE DISPOSE
OF BAD
MEMORIES
HERE.

YARD SALE / SIFTER

                          THE MOTION
                          STUMBLES TO
                          COMPLETE
                          ITSELF

THE PAINTER

```
PINE CONES CRACKLE
FOXES EAT HER CATS
THE WAY BLUE AND GREEN
BLEND TO FORM
NOTHING AT ALL---
```

YARD SALE/ TINTYPE

IF I HAVE LEARNED
ANYTHING
IT IS THAT I CAN NOT
OWN YOU

LOOMING

```
E ]E
]E ]
E ]E
]E ]
```

ALLOWANCE

INVEST IN
THE GOODBYES
ALL
THINGS MUST
UTTER

ITLL BE OKAY

```
D  O  N  T
N        S
O        H
W        N
F  E  A  R
```

NO IT WONT

```
D O N O T
P       A
L       S
E       E
L E A V E
```

FLUSH THAT TAKES

                                        SOFT WOT PATTERN
                                        OF THE PILLOW

ICESTORM

PRETEND
I AM NOT
THINKING
OF YOUR
WAIST

LOVE 1

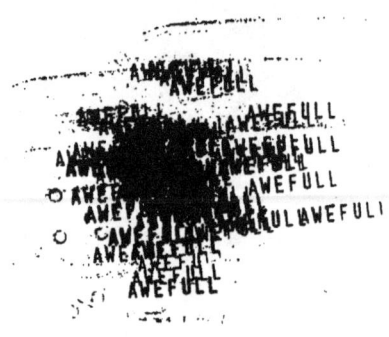

LOVE II

RE-NAMING THE BEACH

'YOU CAN'T THIS
AWAY FROM ME'

YARD SALE/ LANTERN

AN INSECT
IN THE WRIST

WHEN WE WERE BIRDS

IS IT TRUE
THAT ANOTHER'S
SCENT
CAUSES
ABANDONMENT?

UNREMEMBERING 1

HOW THE PATH
MAY NEVER
LICK ITS WOUNDS

UNREMEMBERING 7

                    HOW THE TREE
                    FUMBLES
                    TOWARDS
                    THE MOON

YARD SALE / ANTLERS II

                THE CROWN
                TORN OPEN
                TWO HOLES
                SEE THE LIGHT POUR IN

NORTH

THE FOG IS ROLLING
IN
I FEEL MYSELF
RISE

CONFUSED GHAZAL

                        IN YOUR CHEST?
                        IN YOUR CHEST

                            IN YOUR CHEST?
                            IN YOUR CHEST

                  IN YOUR CHEST?
                  IN YOUR CHEST

                  IN YOUR CHEST?
                IN YOUR CHEST

                IN YOUR CHEST?
                IN YOUR CHEST

              IN YOUR CHEST?
              IN YOUR CHEST

RECEIVE/PERCEIVE

FURY

SORROW, UTTER JOY
SCARED THE LIKES
OF YOU
KNOWING THIS
BRIGHTNESS ABOVE ALL

EYES OR THE LONG STARE

                THE WELLS
                THAT INFINITIZE

FOR THE LAST TIME

                        I WANT TO KNOW
                        WHERE THE LIGHT GOES
                        WHEN IT GOES

YET TO SAY

                              AND
                              MAY NEVER SAY

WAKE ME
WAKE ME

ACKNOWLEDGMENTS

I would like to thank my family for their support and encouragement.

For their generosity, magic, and kindness: Francesca Capone, Mariette Lamson, Liz Welch, Jen Bervin, Sammi LaBue, Courtney Levy, and Sarah Kearsley.

And to Betsy Sholl, for showing compassion to the light and the dark, thank you.

CATIE HANNIGAN is a poet and visual artist whose work incorporates poetry, typography, installation, and photography, with an emphasis on what is simple and deliberate. She has been awarded residencies at Haystack Mountain School of Crafts, Blackfly Writing Retreat, and the Stonecoast Writer's Conference. She lives and works in Portland, Maine. More of her work can be found at www.catiehannigan.com.

❈

COLOPHON

Text is set in a digital version of Jenson, designed by Robert Slimbach in 1996, and based on the work of punchcutter, printer, and publisher Nicolas Jenson. The titles are in Futura.

❀

NEW MICHIGAN PRESS, based in Tucson, Arizona, prints poetry and prose chapbooks, especially work that transcends traditional genre. Together with DIAGRAM, NMP sponsors a yearly chapbook competition.

DIAGRAM, a journal of text, art, and schematic, is published bimonthly at THEDIAGRAM.COM. Periodic print anthologies are available from the New Michigan Press at NEWMICHIGANPRESS.COM.

www.ingramcontent.com/pod-product-compliance
Lightning Source LLC
Chambersburg PA
CBHW031502040426
42444CB00007B/1178